How I Pray for My Friends

by Erik
(with a little help from Jeannie St. John Taylor)

KREGEL Kidzone

How I Pray for My Friends

© 2006 by Jeannie St. John Taylor

Published by Kregel Kidzone, an imprint of Kregel Publications, P. O. Box 2607, Grand Rapids, Michigan 49501.

ISBN 0-8254-3711-3

Printed in China

**To
Andrew Parry**

Most of the time I pray with my eyes closed. That's what I did the time Casper lost his yo-yo. I asked Jesus to help him find it before recess ended, and he *did* find it.

When Sofia skinned her knee, I squeezed my eyes shut so I wouldn't have to look at the blood. I asked Jesus to make it better while I ran to get her mom.

Sometimes Todd says bad words. So at night, I kneel
by my bed and ask God to help Todd understand how
much it hurts Jesus when people say bad words and
use Jesus' name in a bad way.

The day Chuck forgot his lunch, I shared my peanut butter and jelly with him. When we bowed our heads to pray for the food, I asked God to make one little sandwich and an apple be enough to fill up two big boys.

I pray with my eyes open a lot of times, too. I prayed with my eyes open when Laura got the flu. First I asked God to make her cover her mouth and stop sneezing on everyone. Then I asked God to make her well.

At recess, two big girls grabbed
Sofia's bear and played catch with it.
It splashed into a mud puddle and got
all dirty, so I asked God to comfort
Sofia. Then I patted her arm all through
reading time.

Todd made a goofy face behind Ms. Burdon's back. I prayed that Todd would stop acting so mean.

Sometimes I don't know what to pray, so I ask Jesus to help me. When I do that, ideas about what to say just pop into my head, and I'm pretty sure that is Jesus talking to me. I asked him what I should pray after Buzz's parents divorced. He told me to pray for Buzz to understand that the divorce wasn't his fault.

Laura didn't invite Hannah to her party. After I asked Jesus how he wanted me to pray, I got the idea to pray for Laura to be kind. Then I invited Hannah to play with me.

When Todd knocked down my snowman, I knew I should pray for him even though I didn't want to. I said, "Jesus, please forgive Todd and make him be nice. Help me to forgive him, too."

Maddy missed the bus after school one
day. I prayed that she wouldn't feel afraid.
Then I invited her to my house. We ate
cookies while I helped her call her mom.

I asked my mom to help me pray for Casper and Todd because they fight all the time. We knelt at the couch and asked Jesus to help them get along. Now Mom says I'm her prayer partner.

I usually pray in my thoughts, but when I found out Casper's dad lost his job, I prayed out loud. I asked Jesus to help him find work. I prayed every day for weeks, until someone gave Casper's dad a new job.

I thank God for all my friends every day. I tell Jesus I want
them to ask him into their hearts. I think that's the most
important thing I pray, because accepting Jesus is the only way
they can get into heaven. And I sure want them all to be there
with me . . . even Todd.

For Parents

Have you ever noticed that it's sometimes hard to pray for yourself when you are in a difficult situation? I'm convinced that is one of the reasons God wants us to pray for each other. When we're too frightened or confused to pray, God expects our friends to pick up the slack and ask the Father for help on our behalf. And he wants us to do the same for them. Ephesians 6:18 tells us, "Be alert and always keep on praying for all the saints." By "saints" the apostle Paul was referring to other Christians, of course, but God wants us to pray for people who aren't Christians, too. He wants us to pray for all our friends.

Read It Together

As you and your child read about how Erik prays for his friends, you will be reminded of times when similar things have happened in your own family. Did you remember to pray?

Talking It Over

Choose someone you know who is going through a difficult time. If you and your child can't think of a friend with a problem, pick someone mentioned in the news. Talk about how to pray for that person—and others who are experiencing troubles.

Taking Action

Make a pact to pray together, just as Erik and his mom did for Casper and Todd.
List the people that the two of you will pray for. (Adjust the length of the list so that it is appropriate for the age and attention span of your child.) Then set a time each day, or each week, when you and your new prayer partner can pray together. Stick to the schedule, because the Holy Spirit will be waiting to pray with you.

Just for Fun

On a calendar, write down something you can do to help someone you are praying for. Schedule at least one thoughtful act each week for a month. Maybe you could take cookies to them, or make them a card. Whatever activity you choose, make sure that you and your child pray for that person as you do it.